Tech 2.0

World-Changing Social Media Companies

Instagram®

by Craig Ellenport

Tech 2.0

World-Changing Social Media Companies

Facebook®

Instagram®

Reddit®

Snapchat®

Twitter®

WhatsApp®

Tech 2.0

World-Changing Social Media Companies

Instagram®

by Craig Ellenport

Mason Crest

Mason Crest

450 Parkway Drive, Suite D

Broomall, PA 19008

www.masoncrest.com

Printed and bound in the United States of America.

Series ISBN: 978-1-4222-4060-1
Hardback ISBN: 978-1-4222-4062-5
EBook ISBN: 978-1-4222-7729-4

First printing
1 3 5 7 9 8 6 4 2

Produced by Shoreline Publishing Group LLC
Santa Barbara, California
Editorial Director: James Buckley Jr.
Designer: Patty Kelley
www.shorelinepublishing.com
Cover photograph by Syda Productions/Dreamstime.com.

Library of Congress Cataloging-in-Publication Data
Names: Ellenport, Craig, author. Title: Instagram / by Craig Ellenport.
Description: Broomall, PA : Mason Crest, [2018] | Series: Tech 2.0. World-changing social media companies | Includes bibliographical references and index.
Identifiers: LCCN 2018001247| ISBN 9781422240625 (hardback) | ISBN 9781422240601 (series) | ISBN 9781422277294 (ebook)
Subjects: LCSH: Instagram (Firm)--History--Juvenile literature. | Image files--Juvenile literature. | Computer file sharing--Juvenile literature.
Classification: LCC TR267.5.I57 E45 2018 | DDC 770.285/53--dc23 LC record available at https://lccn.loc.gov/2018001247

QR Codes disclaimer:

CONTENTS

KEY ICONS TO LOOK FOR

 Words to Understand: These words with their easy-to-understand definitions will increase the reader's understanding of the text, while building vocabulary skills.

 Sidebars: This boxed material within the main text allows readers to build knowledge, gain insights, explore possibilities, and broaden their perspectives by weaving together additional information to provide realistic and holistic perspectives.

 Educational Videos: Readers can view videos by scanning our QR codes, providing them with additional educational content to supplement the text. Examples include news coverage, moments in history, speeches, iconic moments, and much more!

 Text-Dependent Questions: These questions send the reader back to the text for more careful attention to the evidence presented here.

 Research Projects: Readers are pointed toward areas of further inquiry connected to each chapter. Suggestions are provided for projects that encourage deeper research and analysis.

 Series Glossary of Key Terms: This back-of-the-book glossary contains terminology used throughout this series. Words found here increase the reader's ability to read and comprehend higher-level books and articles in this field.

Tech
2.0

Introduction:
A Global Phenomenon

Quick quiz: If a picture is worth a thousand words, then what is an app that lets you share pictures on your phone worth?

How about one billion dollars?

That's how much Facebook paid to buy the photo-sharing social network Instagram in April 2012. At the time, Instagram had 30 million registered users posting photos and engaging with other users on its platform. Since then, Instagram has exploded to a whopping 800 million users. Forget about the billion dollars from Facebook—experts in the finance community estimate that Instagram is now worth more than *fifty* billion dollars!

Not bad for a company that started out with just two employees and remained pretty small even as it was becoming a global phenomenon. When Facebook bought the company in 2012, there were still only 13 people working for Instagram. The company has since grown to more than 700 employees—but that's still about one employee for every one million Instagram users!

How did Instagram become such a popular app? Social media had already emerged as a major means of communication thanks to established networks such Facebook and Twitter. Instagram's meteoric rise brought a new realization: that visual communication—especially on mobile devices—was the wave of the future.

The concept of visual communication explains why Instagram is so popular on a global scale. It doesn't matter if a picture is worth a thousand words or just a couple. A picture can be understood in any language.

It didn't hurt that Instagram came around just as the boom in smartphones made it easy for anyone to make use of the app. By 2017, more than two billion people around the world had a smartphone. Thanks to Instagram, it

Who Let the Dogs Out?

Social media has always been a popular domain for cute pet photos, so it's no surprise that the very first picture ever posted on Instagram was of a dog. On July 16, 2010, Instagram co-founder Kevin Systrom posted a photo of a golden retriever looking up at the camera.

Systrom was literally the first of millions to post dog pictures on Instagram. Not only are there tons of dog photos on Instagram, there are plenty of dogs with their own Instagram accounts—and some have even become famous.

Maru Taro (@Marutaro on Instagram) has 2.6 million followers! Maru Taro is a fluffy Shiba Inu pooch who lives in Japan and has been posting photos of himself (okay, it's probably his owner who is posting the photos) and has become the most popular dog on Instagram. In fact, a recent survey in Japan revealed that Maru Taro has the second-most popular Instagram account in all of Japan, behind Japanese movie star Kiko Mizuhara.

almost feels as if taking pictures and sharing them is a prerequisite for owning a smartphone.

What's amazing is that the founders of Instagram didn't originally set out to create the world's most popular photo-sharing app. Before Instagram became Instagram, sharing photos was just one small feature of an app that was more about location services. The main idea was that people using the app could "check in" to let people know where they were at any given time.

Back in 2009, when Kevin Systrom and Mike Krieger were brainstorming the idea, the most popular location-services app was something called Foursquare. Not only could users check in at various places on Foursquare, but if they checked in enough times at, for instance, a certain coffee shop, they might earn a free latte there.

As fate would have it, there were many tech companies and startups trying to copy the success of Foursquare. Systrom and Krieger started to think maybe their product would get lost amid the heavy competition in the location services market. The app they were working on was multifaceted—it included many features. So they made a decision: Rather than promote an app that did this, that, and the other thing, let's make an app that focuses on one thing and does that one thing really well.

There were plenty of photo-sharing apps on the market before Instagram launched, and there were several social media networks as well. But Instagram's ability to create a social media network *based* on photo-sharing distinguished it from the competition and set itself up to become one of the leading technology companies in the world.

1

The Origins of Instagram

Kevin Systrom (left) and Mark Krieger, the co-founders of Instagram, first met when they were both students at Stanford University in Northern California.

Systrom grew up in Massachusetts and was always known as a bright kid. His love for programming and computer languages began when he first had access to a computer at home. The year was 1995, and he was twelve years old. Systrom loved playing video games on the computer, especially a game called Doom II. It interested him so much that he tried his hand at editing the different levels found in the game. "That was how I got into it, actually. I'll credit Doom II for everything," he said in an interview, referring to how he first began programming.

His interest in programming did not end with Doom II, though. Systrom learned complex computer languages as his expertise grew. One program he wrote allowed him to boot his friends offline when they were using America Online (AOL), a popular internet-browsing and social-networking tool at the

WORDS TO UNDERSTAND

antics hijinks, acts of mischief

entrepreneurship the process of starting and running a business independently

launch in this case, the first release of an app or program to the public

venture capital money provided by an investor to a young or startup company

time. His online antics actually caused his family's AOL account to be banned! The internet was Systrom's playground, and the expansion of the internet only made him even more enthusiastic about the future.

Meanwhile, Krieger had grown up in a very different area of the world. He was born in São Paulo, Brazil, and did not move to the United States until he was 18 years old, when he became a student at Stanford in 2004.

Stanford University has been home to many startups.

Starting at Stanford

One of the reasons Stanford has attracted so many young entrepreneurs is because of its convenient location. The campus home in Palo Alto, California, is part of a larger area known as Silicon Valley, home to many technology startups. Some of the brightest minds in tech have studied and graduated from this well-known university.

Despite Systrom's interest in computer programming, he didn't actually earn a computer science degree. Instead, he majored in management science and engineering; in fact, he only took one computer science class at the university.

"Stanford is one of the best places to meet engineers who are extremely smart but also well-rounded," he said in an interview.

The management classes got him interested in starting his own company, and he gained valuable experience during his time at Stanford. He was selected to be a part of the Mayfield Fellows, a very selective program for students looking to get involved in growing technology companies. Only about a dozen students are accepted into the program, which helps those students find internships and future jobs in companies both large and small.

One of the first companies at which Systrom interned was Odeo, which eventually re-formed as a new company that developed Twitter after he left. According to Systrom, "Experience is everything," and interning at Odeo was a great way to learn how startup companies worked.

Krieger was learning a lot as well. "We both had really amazing internships then," Systrom said, "that got us to get interested in **entrepreneurship** and get excited about doing it when we got out."

Krieger totally agreed. "A day on the job was worth a year of experience," he said, "and what happens is the collection of experiences and knowledge you can get from those sources are super important."

Working at Odeo gave Systrom the opportunity to meet Mark Zuckerberg, the founder of Facebook. Zuckerberg offered

Facebook founder Mark Zuckerberg played a big role in Instagram's growth.

him a job at Facebook in 2006. Systrom turned down the offer so that he would have time to finish his degree at Stanford. "I'm sure in retrospect it would have been a nice deal, but it's funny where you end up," Systrom said in an interview with *Forbes*. Instead of working for one successful social networking website, he ended up creating his own.

Meanwhile, Krieger was most interested in how humans used computers now and in the future, and that interest has never gone away. He interned at a few well-known companies including Microsoft and Foxmarks, where his skills as a software developer were put to great use. Krieger was learning how larger companies worked, while Systrom continued working at and observing small startups.

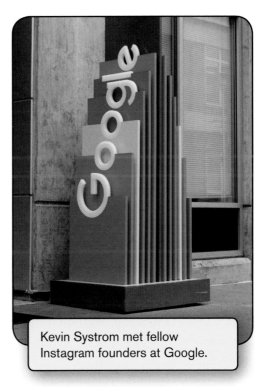

Kevin Systrom met fellow Instagram founders at Google.

Systrom's first job after college was at the internet giant Google, but that job was in marketing, not programming. It wasn't until two years later, when he joined other former Google employees at a startup company called Nextstop, that he eventually took on a job as an engineer.

Krieger followed a slightly different path. Rather than

jumping straight into the workforce, he continued his studies at Stanford and eventually earned a master's degree. After graduation, he joined an instant-messaging firm known as Meebo. He worked there as an engineer for a year and a half. Now the time had come: Krieger and Systrom were ready to join forces to start their own company.

Instagram Inspiration

About a year into working for Nextstop, Systrom began thinking about his own startup project. In order to be successful, he would have to hone his skills as a programmer first. "I started doing more and more engineering at night on simple ideas that helped me learn how to program," he explained. "One of these ideas was combining elements of Foursquare with the elements of Mafia Wars."

Both Foursquare and Mafia Wars were applications that could be used on a mobile device. Foursquare used mobile technology to allow a user to "check in" to places they visited in exchange for rewards. A person who checked in to a local coffee shop might receive a coupon for a discounted coffee, for example. Mafia Wars was a multiplayer game that also functioned as a social network. Players could collect items and compete against each other, all from their mobile devices. Systrom began working on an application he called Burbn that would combine these functions into one app.

Systrom started Burbn on his own, relying on friends and colleagues to test it. While he was working on Burbn, he realized he needed help to truly improve his application. At a party one night, Systrom met two people who worked for **venture capital** firms—companies that invested money in startups they thought could become successful. At this point, Systrom was still working for Nextstop, but he knew if he wanted to give Burbn the attention it deserved, he needed to focus on it completely. "I decided

Startups give presentations to people as they seek funding.

to leave my job to go solo and see if Burbn could be a company." Within two weeks of leaving, Systrom raised $500,000 from the venture capitalist groups he was talking to. He was ready to build his team.

Systrom found a business partner in Krieger, who was very interested in the idea of building an application together. With Krieger's guidance and the funding they had received, Burbn began to take shape.

With Burbn, users could check in to locations (similar to Foursquare), make plans (to check in to locations later), earn

Krieger joined Systrom in founding Instagram.

Instagram's Team of Testers

One of the reasons Kevin Systrom and Mike Krieger knew what users would like is because they tested the application extensively before officially releasing it. "In order to test whether you're working on the right thing or not, you need to put it in front of people," Systrom said. This testing started long before Instagram was even created, and actually began with the first versions of Burbn.

The earliest users of Burbn were confused by all of its features. "We would be in a busy bar and trying to explain to them on our mobile phones and they just wouldn't get it," Systrom recalled. "And that happened enough in front of people outside of our friend group that it was really clear we had to work on something different. Or at least refine the idea."

When Systrom realized that photo sharing would be the main attraction of his product, he reached out to people who were big in design and photography on Twitter and invited them to test it. This proved to be a win-win for Instagram.

"It just so happened that they loved the product and would tweet out about it," explained Systrom. This created interest and demand before Instagram even **launched**.

It didn't hurt that another beta tester was Jack Dorsey, Systrom's friend and the co-founder of Twitter. When Dorsey tweeted about this new app he was testing and enjoying, buzz really started to grow.

Systrom and Krieger had set up a page for people to sign up so they could receive an email when Instagram was ready to launch. When that time came, thanks to Dorsey and Instagram's complete team of testers, there were more than 5,000 people on the mailing list.

points (by hanging out with friends and checking in to locations together), and post pictures. Unfortunately, there was just too much to work with. "It felt cluttered, and overrun with features," Systrom explained. Foursquare was also immensely popular, so it would be difficult for Burbn to compete against it. Any good business owner needs to learn to make tough decisions. That's what Systrom and Krieger had to do now. "It was really difficult to decide to start from scratch," Systrom said, "but we went out on a limb, and basically cut everything in the Burbn app except for its photo, comment, and like capabilities. What remained was Instagram."

The origins of Instagram

The app's name was inspired by photography and an old medium, the telegraph.

The reason they chose to narrow down the application to just photos was because that was the feature most testers liked when they used the original Burbn app. The name of their new app came from a combination of two words: "instant" and "tele-gram." Systrom and Krieger wanted to emphasize the fact that the images were uploaded almost instantly and could be used as a way to communicate between one person and another. Accord-ing to Systrom, another reason he liked the word Instagram is because "it also sounded camera-y!"

On October 6, 2010, at 12:15 a.m., Instagram went live. This was the moment Systrom and Krieger had worked so hard to reach. Exhausted but happy, they headed for bed. "We figured we'd have at least six hours before anyone discovered the app so we could grab some shut-eye," Systrom wrote on the company's blog. But they were wrong. Within minutes, downloads began pouring in from all corners of the globe. Systrom and Krieger were amazed—and overjoyed.

After only a few hours, they had 10,000 users—and that number was growing. "Are we counting wrong?" they wondered.

At the end of the first week after the company's launch, Instagram had been downloaded 100,000 times. Another week passed, and another 100,000 people had downloaded the app.

Instagram was an instant hit, and users were soon sharing selfies.

By the middle of December, the community had grown to a million users.

"We believe it's the beginning of something bigger," Systrom wrote on his blog. "It was both rewarding and humbling to see people embrace Instagram as both a new home on their iPhone—and a new way of communicating visually with people around the world. We believe this is only the beginning."

Systrom and Krieger had come a long way in just a short time.

Text-Dependent Questions

1. What video game first inspired Systrom?

2. What was the name of his first attempt at a startup?

3. Why did the founders retain photography as the key takeaway from their original burbn app?

Research Project

Read more about the app Foursquare and learn its features. What features from there do you see remaining in Instagram? What parts of it do you think could be a successful addition to Instagram? How would you design a logo for Foursquare if it was a new app today?

2

Staggering Growth

During a 2017 interview on *The Today Show*, Mike Krieger explained what he and Kevin Systrom set out to do when they launched Instagram seven years earlier:

"We basically stripped away everything and said, 'Alright, if we want to just make this particular experience of taking a photo, shooting it, being really proud of it and excited to share it, and making that really quick . . . how do we make that incredible?'"

Krieger and Systrom were great problem solvers. As they were preparing Instagram for launch, they recognized that there were three basic problems they needed to solve in order to make Instagram a success:

1. Make photos beautiful. Systrom recalled going on a mini-vacation to Mexico (left) with his girlfriend shortly before Instagram launched. As with any vacation, taking pictures was involved. Systrom's girlfriend noted that existing photo apps at the time all featured filters that would enhance the quality of the photos being taken. "She was like, 'You need to make my photos look as good as all of those guys,'" Systrom recalled. That's when he realized they had to add filters to their product, and they did so in a way that you didn't have to be an expert

WORDS TO UNDERSTAND

milestones significant moments or accomplishments during a period of success

release in this case, a name for information put out to the public officially from a company

spam attack a computer-system hack in which millions of bogus emails are sent to users

photo editor to use them. All users needed to do to apply a filter was click it in the Instagram menu. There were all sorts of filters, ranging from different color tones to grayscale possibilities.

"Needless to say that really helped us take off, because it meant that everyone could take beautiful photos."

2. Allow photos to be shared on multiple networks. As they were building Instagram, Systrom and Krieger knew the top 10 photo apps on the market all had filters, but none had a social component—there was no easy way to share photos. Adding the

Making Instagram work quickly to load photos was a key part of the launch.

social aspect set Instagram apart from other photo apps, but they didn't stop there. Rather than compete directly with other social networks, they made it easy for Instagram photos to be shared on more established networks—like Facebook and Twitter. This was a key factor in Instagram's incredibly fast growth.

3. Upload photos quickly. When Instagram launched in 2010, it took much longer for images to be uploaded on mobile devices than it does today. Systrom and Krieger knew they had to make uploading photos a smooth process, otherwise users would get tired of it. One thing they did to speed things up was to reduce the photo size before it gets uploaded. Amazingly, they did not need any special tech wizardry beyond that; it was all in the delivery. The way they set up Instagram was that users would click to post a photo and then they would type in a caption. As soon as they click to post, the image would begin uploading. So by the time they finish typing in the caption, the upload would be complete. By keeping the user busy instead of just sitting and waiting for the photo to upload, the process flowed naturally.

Reaching one million registered users just four months after launch was incredible, but the **milestones** came fast and furious for Instagram. In June of 2011, it reached five million users. By September of that same year, the number of users doubled to 10 million. That same month, Instagram launched version 2.0 of the app, which included high-resolution photos, four new filters, and the ability to apply filters before taking a picture. Instagram was one year old, and it was already rolling out new features to improve the user experience.

A key moment for Instagram was to create its first app for the Android operating system.

One thing Instagram couldn't do, however, was attract users from the growing base of Android customers. Instagram was named iPhone "app of the year" in 2011 by Apple, but it had yet to offer a version for Android users. That changed on April 3, 2012, when Instagram became available as an app for Android phones for the first time. Within 24 hours, the app got a million downloads.

The Android success kicked off what may have been the most significant month in the history of Instagram. Just a few days after the Android news, Instagram announced a new round of venture capital funding worth $50 million. Financial experts now estimated that the company was worth $500 million.

Mistakes Along the Way

Every company makes mistakes, and Instagram made a very big one in December of 2012.

The social networking website updated its policy to give itself the right to sell any photos uploaded to the website to third parties without notifying the users who uploaded those photos in the first place. This stirred a lot of controversy, with

National Geographic magazine and reality TV star Kim Kardashian (above) being among the loudest voices to complain. As a result of the policy change, many users threatened to leave Instagram to join a different photo-sharing website, such as Pheed and Flickr.

Those websites gained a lot of new users the week Instagram introduced the new policy. A day later, Instagram co-founder Kevin Systrom told users, "Our intention in updating the terms was to communicate that we'd like to experiment with innovative advertising that feels appropriate on Instagram. Instead it was interpreted by many that we are going to sell your photos to others without any compensation. That is not true."

Kevin continued his apology: "It is our mistake that this language is confusing. To be clear: it is not our intention to sell your photos. We are working on updated language in the terms to make this clear."

Fortunately for Instagram, this was a small roadblock to future success. It served as a reminder to Instagram's founders that respecting the rights of its users was an extremely important part of maintaining a growing community.

At that point, Systrom and Krieger could have sold Instagram to another tech giant and gone off to a private island where they'd live in luxury for the rest of their days. Systrom seemed to nip that idea in the bud when he declared they had no plans to sell. His friend Jack Dorsey, the co-founder of Twitter, inquired about buying Instagram. "Thanks, but no thanks," was Systrom's reply.

While Twitter's interest was turned away, someone else reached out and made Systrom an offer he couldn't refuse.

Systrom and Krieger were both very rich thanks to Facebook.

Facebook Moves In

By the end of April 2012, Instagram announced it had 50 million monthly active users—and a new boss: Facebook's Mark Zuckerberg.

Facebook was so enamored with the idea of making Instagram part of its business that they offered Systrom and Krieger a combination of cash and stocks worth a whopping $1 billion. It was more than double what Twitter had offered. More importantly, they were told that Instagram would continue to be run independently from Facebook.

Systrom and his wife Nicole are pictured at a digital event in Germany.

"Millions of people around the world love the Instagram app and the brand associated with it," Zuckerberg said in a company **release**, "and our goal is to help spread this app and brand to even more people."

Systrom viewed the deal more as a partnership than an acquisition, and he recognized that Facebook's large staff of engineers could help Instagram's much smaller team with some of the technical issues that continued to pop up because of the company's growing traffic.

"Facebook has the best tech team in the business and we get to use those assets," Systrom explained in an interview with Bloomberg News. "Every day that went by we were struggling to keep the site up, struggling under our own growth." As an example, Systrom recalled a giant **spam attack** that occurred not long after the Facebook deal.

"We got [Facebook engineers] in there and started using their tools immediately to fight spam," said Systrom. "A lot

Facebook brought new engineering talent to Instagram.

of these things happened immediately after the acquisition and helped the company grow and skyrocket."

Systrom and Krieger were very clear with Instagram users following the Facebook deal that they had no intention of slowing down, and that Instagram would continue as its own product. Within a year of the acquisition, Instagram's monthly users doubled again, hitting the 100 million mark.

Having the resources of Facebook helped Instagram roll out a series of new features. Most notably, on June 13, 2013, Instagram introduced its video-sharing feature, simply called "Video on Instagram." There were even new filters specifically for video.

Instagram basics

"What we did to photos, we just did to video," Systrom said at the announcement.

Most people saw the introduction of video sharing on Instagram as Facebook's answer to rival Twitter, which had bought Vine in 2012. While Vine was an app that allowed users to share 6-second videos, Instagram videos could be as long as 15 seconds.

Systrom denied that the 15-second videos were a clear attempt to compete with Vine's shorter videos. He said they settled on 15 seconds as "an artistic choice."

Adding video capability inspired many Instagram users.

Whether it was art or business—or some combination of the two—didn't really matter. The bottom line was that Instagram was positioned to be one of social media's major players.

Text-Dependent Questions

1. Name one of the three problems the text says Instagram needed to solve.

2. What platform did Instagram join in 2012 that really gave it a huge usership boost?

3. What was one of the benefits of Facebook's purchase of Instagram?

Research Project

Research the 2012 controversy about selling images. Why were people so upset? Do you think they were right? What do you think of Instagram's reaction? Try to write a new policy for Instagram about the proper use of images on their site.

3

Innovative Storytelling and a New Rival

When Facebook bought Instagram in 2012, the company had $0 in **revenue**. This didn't concern Facebook executives, as they were confident that Instagram's huge base of registered users would provide an opportunity to earn money through advertising. In November 2013, designer brand Michael Kors (left) became the company's first official advertiser.

Ads appear on a user's Instagram feed as "sponsored posts." It could be a photo or video, but would have no caption and would have the word "Sponsored" above it. As with other massive social networks, Instagram is able to use **data mining** to target specific ads to specific users based on demographics—where they live, what kind of companies or celebrities they follow.

One thing Instagram wanted to do with advertising was make sure the ads were visually pleasing. They encouraged advertisers to be creative with their ad posts. This made perfect sense for companies looking to reach Instagram users—especially since Instagram posts couldn't include links. You couldn't

WORDS TO UNDERSTAND

analytics the science of using large sets of data to make decisions

data mining examining and studying information to find out specific information, usually about people

nexus the point at which two or more similar things come together

revenue money earned by a company for selling goods or services

just click on a cool ad and be taken to that company's website, so the company has to work harder to make an impression.

"Our aim is to make any advertisements you see feel as natural to Instagram as the photos and videos many of you already enjoy from your favorite brands," Instagram wrote on its blog announcing the new ads. "After all, our team doesn't just build Instagram, we use it each and every day. We want these ads to be enjoyable and creative in much the same way you see engaging, high-quality ads when you flip through your favorite magazine."

Small businesses became adept at using Instagram to reach people.

The Michael Kors ad that was the first sponsored post on Instagram proved to be a good example. Thanks to a tasteful image of a Michael Kors designer watch, the company's Instagram account gained 34,000 new followers in the first 18 hours after it appeared. Within a year of launching the sponsored posts, Instagram began offering companies expanded tools to help them get the most out of advertising on the platform. Companies that ran ads on Instagram could receive data and **analytics** showing them how well a post was received—how many people saw it, how many people liked it, and what kind of comments were posted.

Over the years, as users became more comfortable with the appearance of advertising on their timelines, Instagram gave advertisers even more freedom. Advertisers were allowed to post 30-second videos—twice as long as videos posted by other users—and they were now able to include links to sign up for an email newsletter or visit the advertiser's website.

Reaching to Snapchat

The executive most responsible for launching Instagram's advertising business was Emily White, a former Facebook employee who became Instagram's director of business operations when Facebook bought the company. White did such a great job building Instagram's advertising department that she eventually got hired away by a new social network that was trying to compete with Instagram: Snapchat.

Launched almost two years after Instagram, Snapchat was a mashup of text messaging and photo sharing. Users could send photos to their friends—but the photos would disappear seconds after being viewed. Snapchat became very popular in a very short period of time. Its meteoric rise was quite similar to Instagram's—with the added benefit that Snapchat was most popular with teens and young adults, prime targets for advertisers.

The rise of Snapchat was so much like the rise of Instagram, in fact, that Facebook tried to buy Snapchat a year after it bought Instagram. The difference is that Snapchat turned down Facebook's offer—an astounding $3 billion.

White's experience at Facebook paid off for Instagram.

In the years since Instagram's launch, there have been several other photo-sharing apps trying to capitalize on its success, but it was clear that Snapchat would be Instagram's primary competitor. For what it's worth, Instagram co-founder Kevin Systrom, in a 2016 interview with *Bloomberg News*, would not single out Snapchat.

"I think we are competing against many different services for time and eyeballs, etc.," said Systrom, also noting that Instagram had reached 500 million active users around the world at the time—second only to Facebook and well ahead of Snapchat among social networks. But he also knew he couldn't relax. "We are absolutely not sitting happy, thinking that's going to last forever," he said. "We need to keep innovating, keep introducing new products."

Early on, Instagram's innovations were centered around new filters and other ways to improve photo quality. Whether they admitted it or not, it seemed clear to many that several newer features were introduced as direct responses to the popularity of Snapchat and other competitors.

Some key examples:

Explore: Launched in 2012, Explore had more to do with Twitter than Snapchat. Instagram had already incorporated the use of hashtags, which were made popular by Twitter and made it easier for users to search for posts about a specific subject based on an accompanying hashtag. Instagram's Explore function allowed users to search for posts based on a specific subject or event, with or without a hashtag. It allowed users to discover a world outside of their own follows.

"We believe you can see the world happening in real time through Instagram," Systrom said when Explore was launched. "And I think that's true whether it's Taylor Swift's 1989 tour, which trends on Instagram all the time, or an important moment like a protest overseas, or a march like '*Je suis Charlie*' in Paris [in 2015]. We want to make all of those, no matter how serious, no matter how playful, discoverable and accessible on Instagram. Because at the end of the day, there's no better way to consume what's happening in the world other than images and video. I think Instagram is at the natural **nexus** of both of those."

Instagram Direct: Launched in 2013, Instagram Direct allows users to send private messages to specific people—similar to a text or a Direct Message in Twitter. The ability to send photos and videos in a private message is seen as a clear response to features created by Snapchat.

When Instagram launched Direct, Systrom made it very clear that Instagram was a communications tool more than just a photo app. "Communication is not about photography, necessarily," he said. "If we were about photography we'd be built into cameras, but we're not, we're built into phones."

Gatherings to support 2015 Paris victims used Instagram.

Direct allows users to send a photo or video to one person or as many as 15. Over the years, Instagram has updated Direct to allow users to send text, links, and hashtags, along with the ability to make messages disappear—just like Snapchat.

Hyperlapse: Launched in 2014, Hyperlapse is a stand-alone app that allows users to take time-lapse videos using photo stabilization technology that previously had not been available on mobile devices. Hyperlapse videos can be shared on Instagram.

Sports World Embraces Instagram Stories

Within a year of launching Instagram Stories in 2016, 250 million users were engaging with the storytelling feature. One group in particular that has really taken advantage of Stories' popularity has been professional athletes.

The sports industry is the third-most popular community on Instagram (behind music and entertainment). Athletes have discovered that ephemeral posts—photos and videos that disappear after they are shared with fans—are an easy way to build a closer connection with fans around the world.

The numbers make sense: According to Instagram data, one third of Instagram users identify as sports fans and follow an average of 10 sports accounts each, with an average of eight of those accounts belonging to an athlete. Of those people, 94 percent said they come to Instagram to connect with the personal side of athletes.

"Live on Instagram is one of the biggest immediate megaphones you can use on social," said Will Yoder of Instagram's sports partnerships team in an interview with SportTechie.com. "Instagram Stories allows them to communicate with a younger audience in the way they want to consume content."

It's that younger audience that has led to teams and leagues getting in on the action. NFL team accounts have taken to posting live video on Instagram immediately before and after games. The top two NBA players on Instagram—LeBron James and Stephen Curry (above)—have a combined 52 million followers, and the NBA as a league has truly embraced the platform. Instagram announced that the NBA's combined accounts—league, teams, players and related accounts—have generated 2.5 billion video views.

Using Instagram Stories

Boomerang: Another stand-alone app, Boomerang was launched in October 2015. It allows users to take a one-second burst of five photos that becomes a GIF-like video that plays forwards and backwards. While not an actual video, Boomerang was Instagram's recognition that video sharing on mobile was growing. Being able to share Boomerang loops on Instagram and Facebook was Instagram's attempt to add more viral content.

Stories: In what was seen as the most obvious reaction to Snapchat, Instagram Stories was launched in August 2016. Stories gives users the ability to create a slideshow of photos taken in a 24-hour time period, and the slideshow lives on your timeline before disappearing after 24 hours. Industry insiders accused

Instagram of copying Snapchat—which had a similar functionality that was also called "Stories." Systrom called the criticism "fair," but he also downplayed it, saying that all communication technology companies have similarities.

"You can trace the roots of every feature anyone has in their app, somewhere in the history of technology," Systrom said when Stories launched. Systrom likened it to the automobile industry. Different car models have the same features, but there's enough of a difference in the design or the presentation that leads people to choose one or the other.

While there is little doubt Instagram Stories was influenced by Snapchat, there's also a good chance it was inspired by Instagram's own statistics. Instagram's user base continued to grow, but data showed that users were posting fewer photos. The

Right car for you? Choosing photo apps is a similar process.

thought was that Instagram had become so popular, people were afraid to post images that weren't as beautiful as others.

"Our mission has always been to capture and share the world's moments, not just the world's most beautiful moments," Systrom said. "Stories will alleviate a ton of the pressure people have to post their absolute best stuff." Whether it was motivated by competition from Snapchat or simply the desire to improve its product, the end result of Instagram's innovations was continued growth and popularity. The platform was on its way to reaching a billion users.

Text-Dependent Questions

1. What was Instagram's annual revenue when Facebook bought the company?

2. Name one of the features Instagram added that the text says were designed to help them compete with Snapchat.

3. Name one of the two NBA players the text says have huge Instagram followings.

Research Project

Create a pros and cons chart comparing Snapchat and Instagram. What things work on each app and what do not? What do you think is missing on each? What are the advantages and disadvantages of using each app?

4

A Kinder, Gentler Instagram

nstagram co-founders Kevin Systrom and Mike Krieger prided themselves on creating a social network built on kindness. When the app first launched in 2010, Systrom and Krieger took it upon themselves to delete hateful comments. A few times, they even went so far as to ban users who were seen as "trolls" that were using the service to spread messages of hate or negativity.

As Instagram grew in popularity, such hands-on "policing" of the service became impossible. With that in mind, Systrom and Krieger set out to create new technological advancements that would make Instagram a more welcoming community.

"We believe a lot in giving people the control to make sure that their space feels safe," Krieger said on *The Today Show* in May 2017. "So they can filter out certain words and comments, turn off comments entirely, block people that are making them uncomfortable or just being jerks, to put it really simply, is really important to us."

According to a survey conducted by a British anti-bullying organization, 42 percent of survey responders aged 12–20 reported that they have been bullied on Instagram (left). That same survey found that 70 percent of the

WORDS TO UNDERSTAND

inundated overwhelmed, completely filled with

muzzle a device put on a dog's mouth to prevent it from biting or barking; in this case, a verb meaning to shut down or stop

responders did not think digital platforms were doing enough to prevent bullying.

Systrom had seen if before, but the straw that broke the camel's back came in the summer of 2016. Systrom was in Disneyland, of all places, for an industry event, and he posted a Boomerang video on his Instagram account of himself posing with a bunch of popular Instagram users. After the first few innocent comments on the thread, there followed a barrage of lewd and inappropriate comments aimed at a young girl in the post.

Instagram's headquarters are on Hacker Way in Menlo Park, California.

Systrom returned to Instagram headquarters in Menlo Park, California, and directed his engineering team to find a solution to the bullying problem, a way to put a **muzzle** on all the nastiness. The first big step in this process was a program designed to filter out specific keywords and emojis from comments. They tested it with pop star Taylor Swift's account, which at the time was being **inundated** with rude comments. In particular, Swift bashers took to posting snake emojis on her timeline. Thanks to the new program, the snakes disappeared and users were unable to post new ones.

Instagram helped reduce rude comments toward Taylor Swift.

By the end of 2016, Instagram was able to give users the ability to turn off the commenting tool for specific posts. This was especially beneficial to celebrities and brands on Instagram, since those accounts were frequent targets of harassment. It also was the beginning of what has become a major effort on Instagram's part to silence the haters.

Instagram's "Focus on Well-Being" became a major initiative for the company. Our goal at Instagram is to support well-being by becoming the safest, most supportive and accepting

Celebrities on Instagram

Like the other big social media networks, Instagram is a popular vehicle for celebrities to engage with their fans. Even co-founders Kevin Systrom and Mike Krieger let their fandom show—telling *The Today Show* in 2017 how excited they were when they noticed the first celebrity who registered on Instagram when it launched in 2010. It was rapper Snoop Dogg (right).

Since then, countless celebrities, politicians, and all sorts of famous people have used Instagram to reach the masses. In February 2016, Systrom visited the Vatican to help none other than Pope Francis sign on.

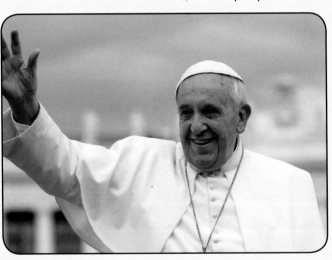

"You realize, these people who are so influential in the world are using our product to get their message out in the world, and that's really special," said Systrom. As of late 2017, Pope Francis (left) had five million followers on Instagram—not bad, but not close to the most followed celebrities on the app.

As of February 2018, six people had more than

100 million followers on Instagram—four are female pop singers, one is a reality TV star, and one is a professional soccer player from Portugal who plays in Spain:

Selena Gomez: 134 million followers
Cristiano Ronaldo: 121 million
Ariana Grande: 118 million
Beyoncé: 112 million
Kim Kardashian: 104 million
Taylor Swift: 104 million

The popularity of these stars can be measured not only in their overall number of followers, but also in how people react to their posts. The 10 photos on Instagram that have received the most likes

come from three accounts—Gomez (left), Ronaldo (above), and Beyoncé.

The photo that holds the record for most likes on Instagram? Beyoncé's pregnancy announcement on Feb. 1, 2017—it received 11.2 million likes. For the record, when Beyoncé announced the birth of her twins in July, the photo got 10.3 million likes—fourth on the all-time list.

platform online," the company wrote in a press release.

"We define our value based on the emotional benefits of the experiences we enable, not simply the utility they provide. We believe the best way to create an environment for you to strengthen your relationships with the people and interests you care about is to invest deeply in becoming a place where you can feel safe, accepted, and supported being your true self."

Social media can lead people toward help if they need it.

The next tool Instagram rolled out, in October 2016, was an interactive program that can reach out to a user in distress. Here's how it works: Suppose you see a friend post something on Instagram that leads you to believe that person is depressed or in need of support. You can send an anonymous report to Instagram, which will then send a message to the person offering information and support.

"These tools are designed to let you know that you are surrounded by a community that cares about you, at a moment when you might most need that," said Instagram chief operating officer Marne Levine when the new program became active.

What was interesting about Instagram's well-being initia-

Cyberbulling news brief

tive is that it combined good intentions—the desire to create a kinder, gentler Instagram community—with some state-of-the-art technology.

In 2016, Facebook—Instagram's parent company—announced the development of a program called DeepText that essentially helped computers "learn." Computers come to understand the meaning of new words based on other words around it. Systrom envisioned a way to use DeepText to his advantage. He formed a team of Instagram employees to pore through a massive

The downside of social media can be the ease of posting negative comments.

amount of commenting on Instagram. The group identified which comments were considered spam and which weren't. By feeding all of this information and text into DeepText, it created a program that could recognize when a comment is meant to be hurtful. No system is perfect, however, and there is always some concern that the program might accidentally block a comment that was not intended to be hurtful.

In 2017, Instagram announced advanced comment control features that can be credited to the use of artificial intelligence.

"The reality is that's going to happen," Systrom said during an interview with *Wired*. "So the question is, 'Is that margin of error worth it for all the really bad stuff that gets blocked?' And that's a fine balance to figure out. That's something we're working on. We trained the filter basically to have a one percent false-positive rate, so that means one percent of things that gets marked as bad are actually good. And that was a top priority for us, because we're not here to curb free speech, we're not here to curb fun conversations between friends. But we want to make sure we are largely attacking the problem of bad comments on Instagram."

Systrom said he felt a responsibility to set a new tone—not only on Instagram but throughout the internet.

"Doing nothing felt like the worst option, so starting to tackle it means that we can improve the world," he said. "We can improve the lives of many young people around the world."

Virtual reality might be one of the next moves for Instagram as it keeps growing.

Still Growing

By all measures, Instagram continues to be one of the leading social media networks in the world. The platform has thrived as a vehicle for nearly a billion users to interact with family and friends, celebrities and athletes, and brands they respect. Instagram has cracked the code on making money without turning away its audience.

In early 2016, the company announced it had 200,000 advertisers. By September of that year, the number reached

500,000. By March 2017, it had one million advertisers and that total doubled to two million just six months later. As of late 2017, the projected advertising revenue for that year was $3.64 billion—and that total was expected to nearly double in 2018.

Not bad for a company that had zero revenue in 2012. While Systrom must be pleased with the financial success, he insists that isn't Instagram's priority.

"We're not in this game to make money," he said. "We're in this game to change the world."

In establishing itself as a primary vehicle for visual communication, Instagram first harnessed the power of photography and then moved on to video. The future of Instagram might just be virtual reality. As Systrom said in a 2017 interview:

This Menlo Park building is where new ideas are born.

"If our vision is to make you feel like you can travel anywhere in the world in a fraction of a second and experience whatever's happening in the world, imagine a day when you can put on a headset and be at a Coldplay concert. Seeing something happen like a big protest or a big riot anywhere in the world or as simple as a friend's wedding. That's the kind of experience we'd like to create, and I think virtual reality in the coming years will play a critical role in seeing that vision come true."

Systrom sees virtual reality and "machine learning" as the logical next step for Instagram. It's a natural extension of what the platform has done since launching in 2010—using technological advancements to create a personal experience—to allow individuals to connect with people and places and things that interest them.

"One thing I've learned through the history of Instagram is the more personalization you have, if we can have an experience

Thanks to Instagram, millions might see a pic like this just after it is taken.

that caters to you the individual, if we know your interests, if we know what you engage with, we can use machine learning and artificial intelligence to make it a much, much better experience for you on Instagram."

Text-Dependent Questions

1. What is the key word the founders used to describe what they wanted Instagram to be?

2. Name two of the celebrities on the list in the text who are among Instagram's top attractions.

3. What does Systrom think are the two next steps for Instagram?

Research Project

Follow one of the famous people in the list on page 52-53. After a few days, write a short report on how you think they are using their Instagram. Are they trying to sell things? Are they trying to make people feel good about the celebrities or themselves? Do you think they are trying to show off or are they truly sharing their feelings?

FIND OUT MORE

Books

Crist, Steve. *The Instagram Book: Inside the Online Photography Revolution.* Los Angeles: Ammo Books, 2014.

Payne, Bridget Watson. *This Is Happening: Life Through the Lens of Instagram.* San Francisco: Chronicle Books, 2013.

Websites

Kevin Systrom Wants to Clean Up the internet
https://www.wired.com/2017/08/instagram-kevin-systrom-wants-to-clean-up-the-internet/

Timeline of Instagram
https://en.wikipedia.org/wiki/Timeline_of_Instagram

Instagram Stats and Facts
http://www.wordstream.com/blog/ws/2017/04/20/instagram-statistics

SERIES GLOSSARY OF KEY TERMS

algorithm a process designed for a computer to follow to accomplish a certain task

colleagues the people you work with.

entrepreneurs people who start their own businesses, often taking financial risks to do so.

incorporate sold shares of stock to become a publicly traded company

innovation creativity, the process of building something new

open-source describing a computer program that can be used by any programmer to create or modify the product

perks benefits to doing something.

startups new companies just starting out.

targeting trying to reach a certain person or thing.

venture capitalists people who invest money in young companies in hopes they will grow greatly in value

INDEX

Photo Credits

AP Photo: Dominic Lipinski via PA Wire 40. Dreamstime.com: Voyagerix 6; Sandra Foyt 12; Erique Calvoal 14; David Johnson 15; imtmphoto 17; Dimarik16 21; Jhogan 22; Lawrence Weslowski Jr. 24; Missjelena 28; CarrieNelson1 29; Peter Ksinan 30; Andre Bujdoso 32; Wavebreakmedia 34; Konstantiv Valikov 38; Maciej Krynica 43; Starstock 44; Stocksolutions 46; Antonio Gravante 48; Wanderlust 51; Jaguarps 52T; Neneo 52B; Natursports 53T; Starstock 53B; Monkey Business Images 54; Fabio Freitas E Silva 56; Andreaobzerova 58; Sundry Photography 59; Syda Prods. 60. Instagram: 18. Newscom: Tobias Haas/Picture Alliance 10; Peter Kneffel/Picture Alliance 31. Shutterstock: Rawpixel.com 26; FashionStock.com 36; Sundry Photography 50. Wikimedia Commons: 8.

About the Author

Craig Ellenport is a veteran journalist with 20 years' experience writing for the web. He has created and managed social media accounts for the National Football League, USA Basketball, and other media outlets.